Science Biographies

Isaac
Newton

Kay Barnham

Raintree is an imprint of Capstone Global Library Limited, a company incorporated in England and Wales having its registered office at 7 Pilgrim Street, London, EC4V 6LB – Registered company number: 6695582

www.raintreepublishers.co.uk
myorders@raintreepublishers.co.uk

Text © Capstone Global Library Limited 2014
First published in hardback in 2014
The moral rights of the proprietor have been asserted.

Edited by Dan Nunn, Adam Miller, and Diyan Leake
Designed by Cynthia Akiyoshi
Picture research by Hannah Taylor and Tracy Cummins
Production by Helen McCreath
Originated by Capstone Global Library
Printed and bound in China

ISBN 978 1 406 27240 6
17 16 15 14 13
10 9 8 7 6 5 4 3 2 1

Barnham, Kay
Newton, Isaac. (Science Biographies)
A full catalogue record for this book is available from the British Library.

Acknowledgements
We would like to thank the following for permission to reproduce photographs: Alamy pp. 7 (© The National Trust Photolibrary), 8 (© Elmtree Images), 10 (© The National Trust Photolibrary), 26 (© World History Archive); Corbis pp. 11 (Historical Picture Archive), 12 (Bettmann), 15 (Jay Nemeth/Red Bull Content Pool); Getty Images pp. 20 (The British Library Board), 21 (Kidstock), 23 (ND/Roger Viollet), 28 (Scott Heavey); Library of Congress Prints and Photographs Division design elements; Photo Researchers (Science Photo Library) pp. 16, 17; Photos.com design elements; Shutterstock pp. 6 (© Artur Bogacki), 13 (© MilanB), 18 (© Frederick R. Matzen), 19 (© Orla), 22 (© Designua), design elements (© Ivanagott, © Sergiy Telesh, © Stephen Coburn, © MilanB, © Morphart Creation; Superstock pp. 4 (SSPL), 5 (Buyenlarge), 9 (Alistair Laming/Loop Images); The Bridgeman Art Library pp. 24 (© tkemot), 27 (National Trust Photographic Library/John Hammond); © The Royal Mint Museum p. 25; © ZCU p. 14.

Cover photographs of Isaac Newton reproduced with permission of Superstock (Christie's Images Ltd) and Shutterstock (Elena Elisseeva).

Contents

Some words are shown in **bold**, like this. You can find out what they mean by looking in the glossary.

Introducing Isaac Newton

Isaac Newton was one of the greatest scientists who ever lived. He studied many different subjects, including **physics**, maths, and **astronomy**. His ideas changed how people thought about the universe.

Newton's most famous discovery was **gravity**. But he also worked out how things move – from the smallest object to the largest planet. He discovered that white light contains the colours of the rainbow. He even invented his own telescope.

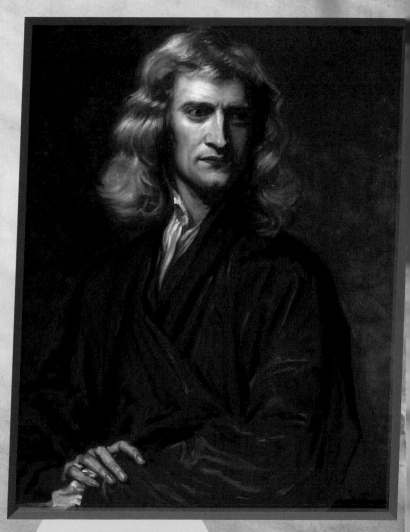

This painting by Godfrey Kneller shows Isaac Newton in 1689, at about the age of 46.

The Renaissance was an exciting time for scientists, as they tried to find out how the universe and everything in it worked. Polish astronomer Nicolaus Copernicus (1473–1543) shocked everyone by saying that the Sun, not Earth, was at the centre of our universe. Italian physicist Galileo Galilei (1564–1642) then showed that Copernicus was right. But until Isaac Newton came along, no one knew that everything in the universe followed the same rules.

What was the Renaissance?

The Renaissance was a time in history when learning once again became as important as it had been in ancient Greece and ancient Rome. It happened between the 14th and the 17th centuries in Europe.

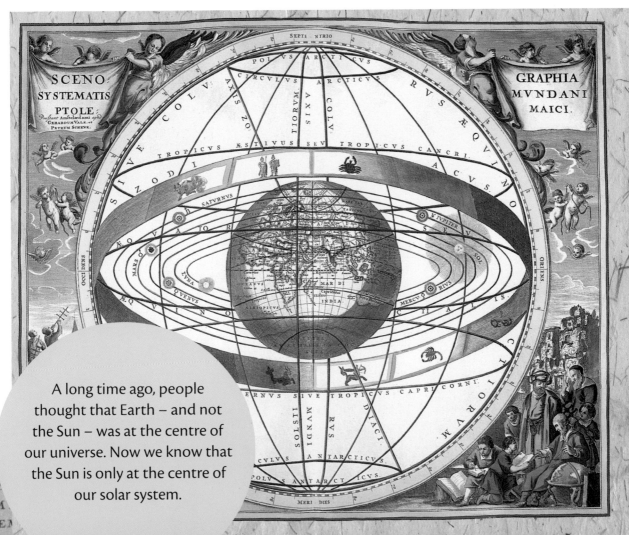

A long time ago, people thought that Earth – and not the Sun – was at the centre of our universe. Now we know that the Sun is only at the centre of our solar system.

Young Isaac

Isaac Newton was born on Christmas Day 1642, near Grantham in Lincolnshire. He was born **prematurely** and was such a tiny baby that he was not expected to live. Against the odds, Isaac survived. Sadly, his father – who was a farmer, also named Isaac – died three months before Isaac was born. Isaac's mother Hannah was now a widow with a new baby.

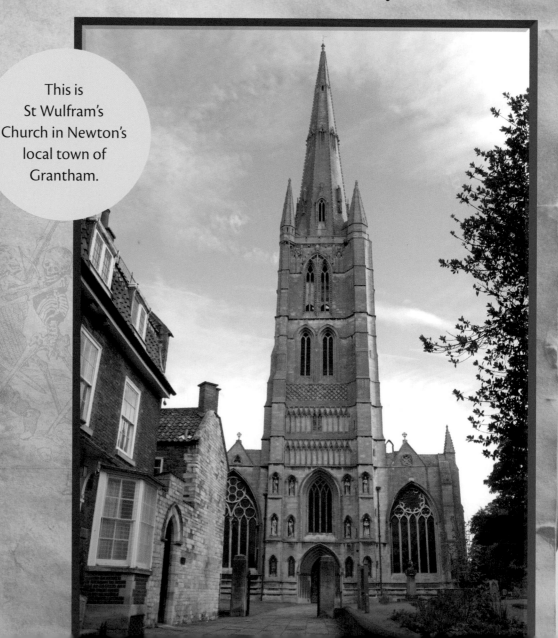

This is St Wulfram's Church in Newton's local town of Grantham.

When Isaac was a very young boy, his mother remarried. Hannah's new husband was a church minister called Barnabas Smith. When Hannah went to live with Smith, she did not take Isaac with her. Instead, he was left behind at the family home, where his grandmother brought him up. Even though his mother returned home when her husband died years later, Isaac never forgave her for leaving him.

This is the hallway of Woolsthorpe Manor, where Isaac Newton grew up. He came from a family of well-to-do farmers.

LANISPHÆRIVM
Sive
BIVM MVNDI
TOLEMA

PTOLEMAICVM
Machina
EX HYPOTHESI
ICA IN PLA

Isaac the student

At the age of 12, Isaac was sent to **grammar school** in Grantham. He was a clever boy, but his mother wanted him to become a farmer and run the family farm. This was a bad idea for two reasons: Isaac did not know how to be a farmer, and he did not *want* to be a farmer. Luckily, his uncle stepped in. He persuaded Hannah that Isaac should continue his education instead.

This is Isaac's school in Grantham. He was bullied there but he decided that he would beat the bullies by scoring higher marks than them.

In 1661, Newton set off for Trinity College, Cambridge. During his first three years at university, Newton worked as a waiter and a cleaner to pay for his studies. But he did so well that he was made a **scholar**. This meant that he would receive funding for the next four years. Newton gave up working so that he could spend all his time studying.

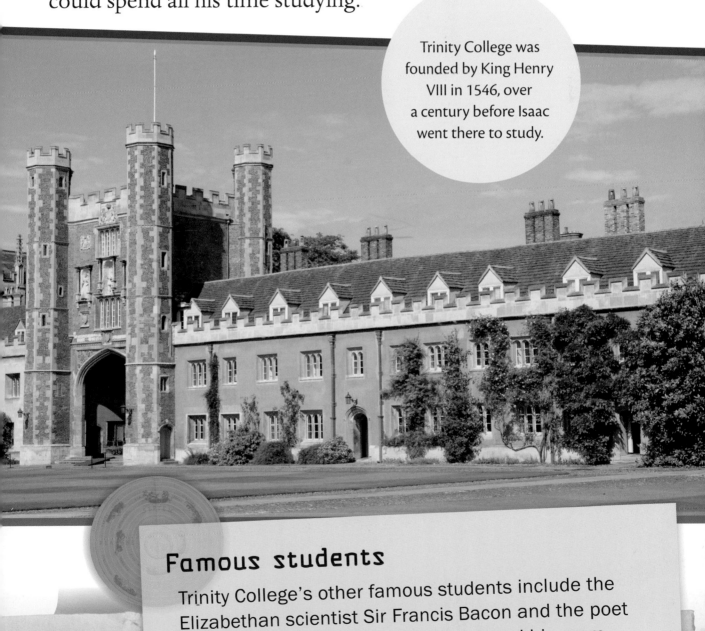

Trinity College was founded by King Henry VIII in 1546, over a century before Isaac went there to study.

Famous students

Trinity College's other famous students include the Elizabethan scientist Sir Francis Bacon and the poet Lord Byron. Byron is said to have shared his room with a pet bear!

Plague!

After four years, Newton graduated from Trinity College. But he wanted to learn even more! Then disaster struck. His studies were interrupted by something very deadly – bubonic **plague**.

The disease had already swept across London, killing thousands of people. Now it had reached Cambridge. To stop the plague spreading through Trinity College, it was closed down at once. Everyone was sent home.

Newton returned home to Woolsthorpe Manor while the plague raged through Cambridge.

THE GREAT PLAGUE

There have been many outbreaks of bubonic plague around the world. It hit England between 1665 and 1666. The outbreak was so bad that it became known as simply the Great Plague. In London, about 100,000 people died of the plague at that time.

Bubonic plague

Bubonic plague is a disease that is carried by fleas. Huge swellings called buboes appear on the sufferer's skin. At first, buboes are red. Then they turn dark purple or black as the skin dies. Today, bubonic plague can be treated with antibiotics, but hundreds of years ago, there was no cure. Two out of every three sufferers died.

During the Great Plague, artists drew pictures to show how gruesome the deadly disease was.

The colours of the rainbow

Newton had escaped the plague, but what was he to do now that he was at Woolsthorpe? He still did not want to be a farmer. So, he decided to study light. Until then, people had thought that the colour white was made of white light, the colour black was darkness, and that all other colours were different mixtures of the two. Newton thought this idea was wrong.

Newton carried out his light experiments in a very dark room.

Newton cut a very tiny hole in a window shutter, just big enough for a tiny beam of sunlight. He put a prism (a triangular piece of glass) in the middle of the room. When sunlight shone through the hole and hit the prism, the white light was split into all the colours of the rainbow.

Newton also showed that it was not just the prism itself adding colour to the light. He directed the rainbow colours through another prism to turn them back into white light.

Try splitting white light into different colours yourself! All you need is a prism and a beam of light, such as a torch.

Newton's apple

One day, Newton sat in the garden at Woolsthorpe and watched an apple fall from a tree and hit the ground. The falling apple made him think. Why did apples always fall downwards and not upwards? He decided that there must be a **force** pulling the apple towards Earth. Newton called this force gravity.

Ouch!

It is sometimes said that the falling apple hit Newton on the head. However, this was probably just made up by people who thought it would make the story more exciting.

Cuttings from Newton's apple tree have been planted all over the world. This one grows at the University of Tokyo, Japan.

GRAVITY

Gravity is the name of the force that pulls two objects towards each other. The larger the object, the greater the **gravitational pull**. Both an apple and our planet have gravitational pull, but because Earth is so much bigger, it has a lot more than the apple. So, both the apple and Earth fall towards each other, but Earth falls a very, very small amount and the apple falls a lot.

Skydiver Felix Baumgartner jumped from a balloon 39 kilometres (24 miles) up in the air in 2012. Earth's gravity pulled him back down to our planet.

NISPHÆRIVM
Sive
MVNDI
MA

AQVARIVS

PTOLEMAICVM
Machina
EX HYPOTHESI
ICA IN PLA

DIA

Newton's telescope

By 1667, the Great Plague was over and Newton returned to Cambridge. Soon, he became a professor of mathematics. His work with glass prisms had shown that they split light into coloured light. Now, he began to wonder if the glass lenses in telescopes split light in the same way. This might be why stars and planets seen through refracting telescopes seemed to have a colourful glow. Newton decided to invent a new kind of telescope that used mirrors instead of lenses to magnify faraway images.

The reflecting telescope worked. When Newton pointed it at the night sky, he clearly saw Jupiter's four moons and the planet Venus.

This composite image shows Jupiter and its four Galilean moons. They are named after the Italian astronomer Galileo Galilei, who discovered them.

The Royal Society

Newton's colleagues were so impressed by his work on reflecting telescopes that they made him a Fellow of the Royal Society, a group of very clever scientists. Since 1660, the Royal Society has done its best to promote science and to encourage research in all areas of science, engineering, and medicine. It was – and still is – a huge honour to become a Fellow of the Royal Society.

This is a copy of the second reflecting telescope that Newton made.

NISPHÆRIVM
ive
MVNDI
IA
AQVARIVS

PTOLEMAICVM
Machina
EX HYPOTHESI
ICA IN PLA

How planets move

Newton realized that the same force that pulled the apple towards Earth might pull larger objects, such as planets, towards each other, too. Soon, he had developed a way of describing how the Moon **orbits** Earth.

Earth's gravity pulls the Moon towards our planet. This means that the Moon is always falling towards Earth. But because the Moon is also travelling sideways, it never reaches Earth. Instead, it travels round and round our planet in a never-ending circle called an orbit.

Once he had described how the Moon orbits Earth, Newton could show how the planets in our solar system orbit the Sun, too. He proved beyond doubt that Earth orbited the Sun and not the other way round.

Newton said that all the planets in our solar system **revolved** around the largest object, which was the Sun. Earth could not be at the centre of the solar system because it was not the biggest thing in it.

Newton's laws of motion

In 1687, Newton published one of the most important books in the history of science. It was called *Philosophiæ Naturalis Principia Mathematica*. In this book, Newton wrote about his work on gravity. He also wrote about his three laws of motion. These laws describe how different forces make objects move, change direction, or stop.

PHILOSOPHIÆ
NATURALIS
PRINCIPIA
MATHEMATICA.

Autore *JS. NEWTON*, *Trin. Coll. Cantab. Soc.* Matheseos Professore *Lucasiano*, & Societatis Regalis Sodali.

IMPRIMATUR·
S. PEPYS, *Reg. Soc.* PRÆSES.
Julii 5. 1686:

LONDINI,
Jussu *Societatis Regiæ* ac Typis *Josephi Streater*. Prostant Venales apud *Sam. Smith* ad insignia *Principis Walliæ* in Cœmiterio D. *Pauli*, aliosq; nonnullos Bibliopolas. Anno MDCLXXXVII.

Newton's famous book is usually just known as *Principia*.

NEWTON'S FIRST LAW

An object will carry on moving unless something stops it or changes its direction and a **stationary** *object will stay still unless something makes it move.* For example, a football will not move unless someone kicks it.

Newton's second law

*Force is equal to the **mass** of an object multiplied by its **acceleration**.* This calculation allows us to work out the answers to lots of questions, including how much force is needed to push an aircraft of a certain weight through the air at a certain speed.

Newton's third law

*For every action, there is an equal and opposite **reaction**.* For example, if a girl on a scooter pushes her foot backwards, the scooter will move forwards.

Making a scooter move forwards is a way of demonstrating Newton's third law of motion.

NISPHÆRIVM
Sive
C MVNDI
MA

AQVARIVS

PTOLEMAICVM
Machina
EX HYPOTHESI
ICA IN PLA

DIA

Newton the mathematician

As well as his work on light, motion, and gravity, Newton also studied a type of maths called **calculus**. In the 17th century, this was a popular topic, and Newton was not the only one trying to find out how calculus worked. The German mathematician and thinker Gottfried Wilhelm von Leibniz was also very interested in calculus.

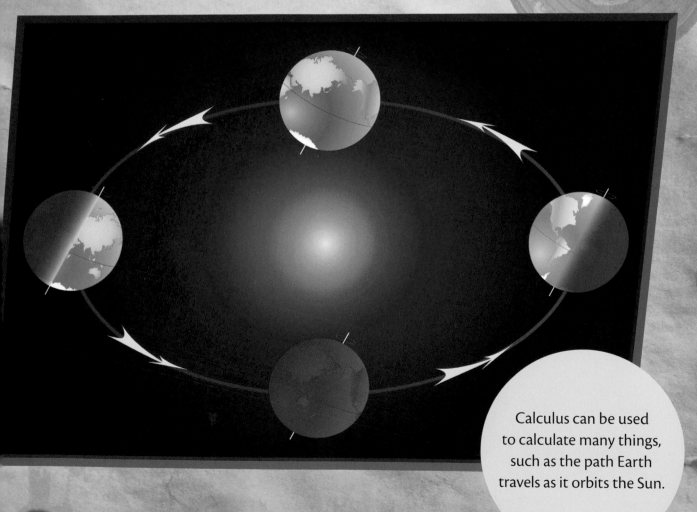

Calculus can be used to calculate many things, such as the path Earth travels as it orbits the Sun.

WHO INVENTED CALCULUS?

Newton and Leibniz each worked alone and in completely different ways. Yet they both came up with the idea of calculus. Now there was a problem. Which one of them had invented it? Newton and Leibniz quarrelled bitterly. The Royal Society decided that Isaac Newton had invented calculus. However, Newton had a lot to do with this decision. Many years later, it was decided that both men had thought of one of the most important mathematical ideas ever. Finally, Leibniz was given the credit he deserved.

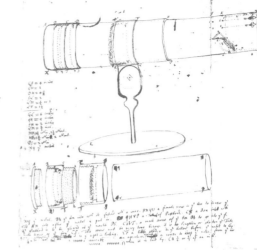

Gottfried Wilhelm von Leibniz (1646–1716) died before the argument over who had invented calculus was settled.

LANISPHÆRIVM
Sive
BIVM MVNDI
TOLEMA

AICVM
hina

EX HYPOTHES
ICA IN PLA

What Newton did next

Newton became a Member of Parliament, but he did not enjoy politics. In 1696, he was made Warden of the **Royal Mint**. Three years later, he became Master of the Royal Mint. He was in charge of making all of the country's new coins. It was also his job to catch **counterfeiters** and cheats.

This is what the Houses of Parliament looked like in Newton's time. They were destroyed in a fire in 1834 and had to be rebuilt.

Newton and the Royal Mint

In the late 1600s, the value of a coin was the same as the cost of the silver used to make it. But it was difficult to make silver coins that were all exactly the right weight. If they weighed too much, the silver in the coin was then worth more than the face value of the coin itself. Dishonest goldsmiths could melt the coins and sell the silver for more money. Newton beat the cheats by finding a way to make coins that were exactly the right weight. Experts think that Newton may have saved the country as much as £10 million in today's money.

This set of weights was used to make coins in the Royal Mint in Newton's time.

Sir Isaac Newton

At the beginning of the 18th century, Newton received two great honours in recognition of his work and scientific discoveries.

The first happened when he was elected President of the Royal Society in 1703. Two years later, he was knighted by Queen Anne and became Sir Isaac Newton. He was only the second scientist ever to become a knight.

Queen Anne knighted Isaac Newton in 1705. She ruled from 1702 until 1714 and became the first monarch to reign over Great Britain, after the kingdoms of England and Scotland were united in 1707.

LAST YEARS

Throughout his life, Newton tried – and failed – to find a way to turn lead into gold. He carried out many experiments using dangerous chemicals, and as he grew older, he may have suffered from **mercury** poisoning.

Newton spent his final years in Winchester, where he lived with his niece and her husband. He remained President of the Royal Society until his death in 1727.

This portrait of Isaac Newton was painted sometime between 1709 and 1712.

LANISPHÆRIVM
Sive
IVM MVNDI
OLEMA

PTOLEMAICVM
Machina
EX HYPOTHESI
ICA IN PLA

After Newton

In his lifetime, Newton did so much to further science that it is hard to imagine what our world would be like today without his ideas and discoveries. There is even a unit of measurement – the newton – named after him. The newton is used to measure force.

Newton's ideas were celebrated at the London 2012 Paralympic Games. A huge golden apple starred in the opening ceremony. It was a way of remembering Newton's discovery of gravity.

Timeline

1642 Isaac Newton is born near Grantham, on Christmas Day

1646 Isaac's mother marries Barnabas Smith

1655 Isaac goes to school

1660 The Royal Society is founded

1661 Newton goes to Trinity College, Cambridge

1664 Becomes a scholar

1665 Completes his university degree; returns to Woolsthorpe to escape the Great Plague

1666 Sees an apple fall from a tree, and this inspires him to think about gravity

1667 Returns to Cambridge and becomes a Fellow of Trinity College

1669 Becomes a professor of mathematics

1671 Shows his telescope to the Royal Society

1672 Becomes a Fellow of the Royal Society

1686 Finalizes his ideas about gravity

1687 Newton's *Principia* is published

1689 Newton becomes the Member of Parliament for Cambridge University

1696 Becomes Warden of the Royal Mint; moves from Cambridge to London

1699 Becomes Master of the Royal Mint

1703 Becomes President of the Royal Society

1704 Publishes *Opticks*, a study of refraction and light

1705 Becomes Sir Isaac Newton

1727 Sir Isaac Newton dies on 20 March

Glossary

acceleration moving more quickly

astronomy study of space and everything in it

calculus type of maths that allows people to work out the answers to very complicated sums about change

counterfeiter someone who makes copies of things and then pretends they are the real thing

force something that changes an object's movement

grammar school school that accepts pupils based on their ability

gravity force that pulls things towards each other

mass how much matter is in an object. Mass is measured in kilograms.

mercury silvery-white chemical that was once used in thermometers

orbit path an object travels when it goes round and round something

physics type of science that studies matter and energy

plague dangerous disease that is very easy to catch

prematurely too early

reaction force that happens as a result of another force

revolve spin round and round

Royal Mint company that has the right to make coins for the United Kingdom

scholar someone who receives money to continue studying

stationary not moving

Find out more

Books

Can you feel the Force?, Richard Hammond (Dorling Kindersley, 2010)

Isaac Newton (Giants of Science), Kathleen Krull (Puffin Books, 2008)

Isaac Newton and His Falling Apple (Horribly Famous), Kjartan Poskitt (Scholastic, 2011)

Isaac Newton and the Laws of Motion (Graphic Library: Inventions and Discovery), Andrea Gianopoulos (Raintree, 2011)

Websites

www.sciencekids.co.nz/sciencefacts/scientists/ isaacnewton.html
Find out lots more about Newton on this website.

www.sciencemuseum.org.uk/onlinestuff/People/Isaac%20 Newton%2016431727.aspx
Read a biography of Newton on the Science Museum website.

Place to visit

Woolsthorpe Manor
Water Lane
Nr Grantham
NG33 5PD

www.nationaltrust.org.uk/ woolsthorpe-manor
You can visit Woolsthorpe Manor, Newton's childhood home.

Index